THE PERSONAGE OF MAN

The Deeper Things of God Series • Book Two

THE PERSONAGE OF MAN

*An In-depth Look at the Express Image Creature
Known of as Man . . .
That Declaration of Creation which is more excellent
Than all of the Angelic Hosts or Other Creatures
That are also products of Moral Creation.*

Robert E. Daley

The Larry Czerwonka Company, LLC
Hilo, Hawai'i

Copyright © 2015 by Robert E. Daley

All rights reserved. No part of this book may be reproduced or transmitted in any form or by any means, electronic or mechanical, including photocopying, recording or by any information storage and retrieval system, without written permission from the author and the publisher.
For information email info@thelarryczerwonkacompany.com

First Edition — June 2015

This book is set in 14-point Garamond

Published by: The Larry Czerwonka Company, LLC
http://czerwonkapublishing.com

Printed in the United States of America

ISBN: 0692473211
ISBN-13: 978-0692473214

The cover image is titled
"Black Marble—Asia and Australia"
flickr.com/photos/24662369@N07/8246893143/
and is a composite assembled from data acquired by the Suomi NPP satellite in April and October 2012.
NASA is not connected with nor do they endorse this book in any way.

All scriptures used in this work are taken from the
King James Version of the Scriptures.

BOOKS BY **ROBERT E. DALEY**

A Case for "Threes"
A Simple Plan . . . of Immense Complexity
Armour, Weapons, And Warfare
from Everlasting to Everlasting
Killer Sex
Life or Death, Heaven or Hell, You Choose!
Raptures and Resurrections
Short Tales
So . . . What Happens to the Package?
Study and Interpretation of The Scriptures Made Simple
Surviving Destruction as A Human Being
The Gospel of John
The Gospel of John (Red Edition)
The League of The Immortals
The New Testament - Pauline Revelation
The New Testament - Pauline Revelation Companion
"The World That Then Was . . ." & The Genesis That Now Is
What Color Are You?
What Makes A Christian Flaky?
What Really Happened to Judas Iscariot?
Who YOU Are in Christ . . . RIGHT NOW!

The Enhancement Series

#1 Book of Ecclesiastes
#2 Book of Daniel
#3 Book of Romans
#4 Book of Galatians
#5 Book of Hebrews

The Deeper Things of God Series

#1 The Personage of God
#2 The Personage of Man
#3 The Personage of Christ

Contents

The Immutability of Counsel **1**

The Study of Man **7**

Prior to Man **11**

The Creation of Man **36**

The Hope for Man **49**

The Deterioration of Man **59**

Fallen Man's Condition Today **73**

THE PERSONAGE

OF MAN

The Immutibility of Counsel

Within a tract written by a man named Winkie Pratney, who is associated with the Last Days Ministries in Lindale, Texas, the mathematical precision of the Scripture is demonstrated through the work of a young Russian Harvard graduate named Ivan Panin, which was begun by Mr. Panin in 1882. Mr. Pratney's presentation is quite impressive and impacting. He goes on to say:

"The whole Bible is like this. I am just taking one small chunk of it and dong it in detail. Every paragraph, passage and book in the Bible can be shown to be constructed in the same marvelous way. What kind of fantastic collaboration between the disciples could have produced this structure without computers? How could mere fishermen and tax-collectors produce this kind of incredible structuring and design? What is crazy is that Mark is a Roman, Luke a Greek, and Matthew a Jew, but they all wrote with the same pattern. Each one wrote with their own unique flavor. Mark's style is different, but the pattern is the same right through! So who wrote it? One Mind, one Author... one God... many different writers, but one Writer. Can you imagine what kind of Mind would do this and not even care if you ever found out? What I want you to see is how smart God is! These are not just words, it's an incredible

mathematical pattern. It dances with its own poetry in mathematics. A computer would go into raptures over this! It's like a building where every piece joins perfectly into each other. And what is wild, is you can't pull even **one** *word out, without damaging the whole pattern. So the Bible carries within itself, a self-checking, self-verifying protection factor. If a person comes along and says I don't like this one, the whole pattern falls apart. This cannot be found in any other religious 'holy' book in the world."*

* * *

On March 20, 1969, at a meeting of the Pediatric Society, a man named Dr. Richard L. Day (who had been an instruction professor since 1935) and had just finished his term as National Medical Director of Planned Parenthood. Moreover, was currently a professor of pediatrics at the Mount Sinai School of Medicine, and who was considered an **insider** within something called **The Order** was quoted as saying:

"You will forget most or much of what I am going to tell you tonight . . . the old religions will have to go . . . especially Christianity. Then a new religion can be accepted for use all over the world.

It will incorporate something from all of the old religions to make it more easy for people to accept and feel at home. Most of the people will not be too concerned with religion. They will realize that they do not really need it.

In order to do this, the **Bible** *will be changed. It will be rewritten to fit the new religion.*

Gradually, **key words** *will be replaced with new words having various shades of meaning.*

Then the meaning attached to the new word, can be close to the meaning of the old word . . . and as time goes on, other shades of meaning for that word, can be emphasized . . . and then gradually that word replaced with another word.

The few who do notice the difference will not be enough to matter . . . And, the churches will help us!"

* * *

It was stated that the idea within this calculated assault upon the Word of God, is that everything within the Scripture does not need to be rewritten . . . just certain **key words** to be replaced by other words.

The variability in meaning attached to any word can be used as a tool to change the **entire** meaning of the Scripture, and, therefore, make it acceptable to this *new* religion. Most of the people will not even know the difference.

It was also stated that Dr. Day was concerned that if what he had stated within that relaxed environment ever really became publically known, that his days would be numbered. Within just a few short months, Dr. Day was dead.

* * *

The whole of this study of The Deeper Things of God finds its basis within the unchanging Word of God, utilizing only the King James Version Translation of the Bible—and no other translation version will be acceptable for use within this study.

* * *

The supreme authority on the subject of God is God Himself. He has granted unto us *"**all things** that pertain unto life and godliness, through the knowledge of him that hath called us to glory and virtue."* *(II Peter 1:3b)*

Jesus of Nazareth said, *"**Sanctify them through thy truth: thy word is truth.**"* *(John 17:17)*

Therefore, we will rely totally upon the written Word of God and upon the Word-of-God-supported, Holy Spirit revelation, in the presenting of spiritual truth and existence realities.

* * *

"The Law of the Lord is perfect, converting the soul: the testimony of the Lord is sure, making wise the simple.

The statutes of the Lord are right, rejoicing the heart: the commandment of the Lord is pure, enlightening the eyes.

The fear of the Lord is clean, enduring for ever: the judgments of the Lord are true and righteous altogether.

More to be desired are they than gold, yea, than much fine gold: sweeter also than honey and the honeycomb.

Moreover by them is thy servant warned: and in keeping of them there is great reward." (Psalms 19:7-11)

* * *

"To the law and to the testimony: if they speak not according to this word, it is because there is no light in them." (Isaiah 8:20)

* * *

"So shall my word be that goeth forth out of my mouth: it shall not return unto me void, but it shall accomplish that which I please, and it shall prosper in the thing whereto I sent it." (Isaiah 55:11)

* * *

"For the word of God is quick, and powerful, and sharper than any two-edged sword, piercing even to the dividing asunder of soul and spirit, and of the joints and marrow, and is a discerner of the thoughts and intents of the heart." (Hebrews 4:12)

***

"Wherein God, willing more abundantly to show unto the heirs of promise the immutability of his counsel, confirmed it by an oath:

That by two immutable things, in which it was impossible for God to lie, we might have a strong consolation, who have fled for refuge to lay hold upon the hope set before us." (Hebrews 6:17-18)

***

"We have also a more sure word of prophecy; whereunto ye do well that ye take heed, as unto a light that shineth in a dark place, until the day dawn, and the day-star arise in your hearts:

Knowing this first, that no prophecy of the Scripture is of any private interpretation.

For the prophecy came not in old time by the will of man: but holy men of God spake as they were moved by the Holy Ghost." (II Peter 1:21)

***

The testimony of the Word of God applies to every subject or situation that we may encounter. The Word of God is our foundation . . . the Word of God is the bottom line . . . the Word of God is the end of the story . . . the Word of God is what God is. Everything that we will be looking at within our studies will find its foundation within the Word of God.

The Study of Man

The *New Webster's Dictionary* defines:
Man *1)n. a human being; esp.: an adult male human 2) a man belonging to a particular {**Creation**} category (as by birth, residence, membership, or occupation) 5) the compound idea of infinite Spirit: the spiritual image and likeness of God: the full representation of Mind*

Man is a *finite* being, which means that he is restricted by natural and supernatural limitations.

A *finite* being **cannot** fully comprehend the *infinite* Being because there is no common point of reference to measure from, within the everlasting contexts that exist.

* * *

"When I consider thy heavens, the work of thy fingers, the moon and the stars, which thou hast ordained;

What is man, that thou art mindful of him? and the son of man, that thou visitest him?

For thou hast made him a little lower than God, and hast crowned him with glory and honor.

Thou madest him to have dominion over the works of thy hands; thou hast put all things under his feet:

All sheep and oxen, yea, and the beasts of the field;
The fowl of the air, and the fish of the sea, and whatsoever passeth through the paths of the seas." (Psalms 8:3-8)

As we begin our study of MAN, it is appropriate that we consider the same question as did the psalmist King David. The answer, of course, is found within the Word of God.

"And God said, Let us make man *on the inside of his being* **in our** *own* **image,** *and on the outside of his being* **after our** *own* **likeness: and let** *all of* **them have dominion**, *power, and authority* **over** *all of* **the fish of the sea, and over** *all of* **the fowls of the air, and over** *all of* **the cattle** *in the fields***, and over all** *of the whole* **earth, and over every** *single* **creeping thing that creepeth upon the earth."** *(Genesis 1:26)*

An *enhanced* version of the Genesis verse above conveys the divine intended thought behind the declared statement that God made, when the time came to bring into existence a superior created creature that would be as close as possible to being like the Personage of God Himself as could be achieved.

It should be an understood *no-brainer* that within this singular functioning, created universe, there is no Being currently existing who is greater than the One and only, who brought forth the whole of the universe in the first place. The Person of God is the Supreme Being. The Person of God is the bottom-line Source. The Person of God is the Almighty Creator. And any ideas or postulations or proposals to the contrary, are those notions that emanate forth from a sin-defiled, two-dimensional, delusional mindset that purposely avoids the Record of Truth in order to impose their self-exalting positions of uncertainty upon the unsuspecting associate dupes within Mankind.

There are indeed other moral creations that God has brought forth before Man became the center of attention. The *Creation Category #2* of intelligent, moral, free-willed beings would be the *Angelic Hosts* of heaven, and the *Creation Category #3* constituency of intelligent, moral, free-will beings are the *Other Creatures (Romans 8:39)* that occupy various locales within this universe, and some of which, were the first inhabitants of this planet Earth.

But *Man* and *Man* alone holds the *Creation Category #1* position and is the only moral created creature that the God of Creation brought forth specifically ***in*** His own ***image*** and ***after*** His own ***likeness***. *(Genesis 1:26)* Man was to be unlike any of the other moral beings that God had created. Man was to be without precedent. Man was destined, right from the beginning, to rule.

Prior to Man

*I*n *the Beginning* of the creation process, God brings forth the *Basic Creation Elements* of *Air, Water, Soil, and Fire*. The first three of these Basic Creation Elements are constructive. They are going to be used in the construction of galaxies, and stars, and planets . . . and specifically will be needed for the amenities that will come forth on various planets during the formation and development of this universe. *(Jeremiah 1:12)*

Once the universe is in the active process of progressive development, divinely calculated inanimate creation occurred, within focused preparation of the animate moral creation that would soon follow. God ordained, intelligent, moral associates, of the *Creation Category #2, Angelic Hosts* are then created, that will be utilized in the fabricating and constructing of various cities and residences on various planets, and additionally, will be attending to the other myriad of nuances of universal growth and progression.

Free-will gifting is accompanied by personal visionary desires, and granted morality includes a substantially intelligent thought-process. Primarily, the *Basic Creation Element* of *Air* is utilized within the formation of these creatures belonging to the heavenly *Angelic Hosts* compliment of beings, as can be determined by the following Scriptures:

"By the word of the Lord were the heavens made; and all the host of them by the breath of his mouth." (Psalms 33:6)

* * *

"For he spake, and it was done; he commanded, and it stood fast." (Psalms 33:9)

* * *

"Praise ye the Lord. Praise ye the Lord from the heavens: praise him in the heights.

Praise ye him, all his angels: praise ye him, all his hosts,

Praise ye him, sun and moon: praise him, all ye stars of light.

Praise him, ye heavens of heavens, and ye waters that be above the heavens.

Let them praise the name of the Lord: for he commanded, and they were created." (Psalms 148:1-5)

* * *

After a designated period of time, which is incalculable, lower, gravity-bound, *Creation Category #3* constituencies of *Other Creatures* (Romans 8:39) are then brought onto the scene in various universal locales, utilizing primarily the *Basic Creation Element* of *Soil*.

There is no Scriptural support of either the heavenly *Angelic Hosts* or of the terrestrial *Other Creatures* having received any reproductive-permission from God. So whether the original creation of them was uniquely individual or of an en masse nature is unsubstantiated at this time, at least by this author.

From this point onward within our studies of the Personage of Man, and definitively focusing in on this particular planet named Earth, these *Other Creatures* are noted as being intelligent, moral, and of a free-will volition. They also can fabricate and construct cities *(Jeremiah 4:26)* and purpose to separate themselves into various nations. *(Isaiah 14:12)* When the judgment occurs for all of the rebellious participants within the *Angelic Probationary Period*, the judgmental flood waters that cover this planet Earth *(Psalms 104:6)* drown and destroy the physical bodies of the *Other Creatures*, and they become the disembodied evil spirit beings that today we refer to as *Demons*.

One of the numerous judgmental actions that occurred concerning the planet Earth, at the conclusion of the *Angelic Probationary Period*, is the blocking of all ambient light sources that have an effect upon this globe. *(Jeremiah 4:23)* That blocking action causes the recently released flood waters to freeze, and an Ice Age period commences to occur, and as of yet, there exists no area of locale that either of the rebellious *unholy Fallen Angels* nor of the disobedient *Other Creatures* may be definitively assigned to for continued abiding.

* * *

Special Notation: *There is no Scriptural support anywhere of the Human-proposed idea of "annihilation from existence." Once a creature is either originally created or permissively reproduced, they are in the reality of existence to stay. Their particular eternal abiding locale, within their existence, is what is in question.*

* * *

"For a fire is kindled in mine anger, and shall burn unto the lowest hell, and shall consume the earth with her increase, and set on fire the foundations of the mountains." *(Deuteronomy 32:22)*

"Then shall he say also unto them on the left hand, Depart from me, ye cursed, into everlasting fire, prepared for the devil and his angels:" *(Matthew 25:41)*

* * *

Prior to the first universal rebellion of intelligent, free-willed, moral creation there was no valid reason for a God of Love to be angry. Prior to the first rebellion of intelligent, free-willed, moral creatures, there was no valid reason for a God of Love to carve-out, or *prepare* a locale for incarceration of disobedient and rebellious creation—even though Foreknowledge is aware of the disobedient actions that will occur. *(Isaiah 46:10)* However, the time has now come, and there can be no further delay.

The World of Departed Spirits . . . or *The Region of the Damned* . . . or *The Nether World* (in addition to *Hell*) are just a few of the names that have been ascribed to the *prepared* locale that the disobedient and contentious creatures within this universe will remain consigned to forever more.

They have consciously, willingly, and knowingly chosen to rebel against the living God—and God has given unto them a viable opportunity to change their minds—but they have adamantly refused to accept and benefit from that offer and now they are relegated to remain separated from God, and from all of the other intelligent, moral, free-willed creations that God has graciously brought forth for His pleasure.

The location of Hell was originally prepared for the Devil and his angels, *(Matthew 25:41)* but when Mankind comes onto the scene (and for a second time free-will rebellion can occur again) the locale will be sufficient to house the Human, **"vessels of wrath fitted to destruction"**, as well. *(Romans 9:22)*

At the outset, the entire locale of *Hell* is void.

There are five separate compartments that are prepared in line with Foreknowledge, but the actual bringing forth of the locale was originally an after-the-fact preparation caused by necessary judgment. *(Deuteronomy 32:22; Matthew 25:41)*

The locale of *Hell* has a layered construct. Two of the compartments are at an upper-level (two of the compartments are on a first-floor level) and one of the compartments is in the basement.

1) Paradise *(unto the Gentile)* **. . . Abraham's Bosom** *(unto the Jew)*:

"And it came to pass, that the beggar died, and was carried by the angels into Abraham's bosom: the rich man also died, and was buried;" *(Luke 16:22)*

"And Jesus said unto him, Verily I say unto thee today, Shalt thou be with me in paradise." *(Luke 23:43)*

The first spiritual reality that we need to understand is that this story of the rich man and the beggar is **not** a parable. Specific people are not ever named within a parable as Lazarus is named within this story. Moreover, Jesus is not using familiar objects that the people around him would be able to understand, to convey a spiritual truth. Jesus is telling us of an actual incident that occurred, and giving us an insight into the realm that we cannot see with our physical eyes at this present time.

Secondly, we need to adjust *uninspired punctuation* to reflect the correct intended thought and declaration in line with the actual truth. Jesus did not go into the *Paradise* compartment on the very same day that he died. Jesus went where I would go if I was the one hanging on the cross instead of him, and paying for my sins.

Paradise, as it was known by the Gentiles, or *Abraham's Bosom*, as the Jews knew it, is an upper-level compartment, and is the first one that we shall look at. It is positionally located somewhere under the crust of this planet.

If we have ever seen a rock quarry, or are familiar with the dirt and rock composite make-up of this planet, then we know that giant caverns are not simply just indiscriminately scattered in various locales under the outer crust of this Earth. There are certain caves and caverns such as the Carlsbad Caverns that are of a *natural phenomenon* it is true. However, the *Region of the Damned* is an area that was purposely and meticulously prepared by God. So there is at least one, generally large location that has been established concerning this Spiritual-Housing-Project for the spiritually-criminally condemned. Additionally, there are at least two entrances to this housing project that shall become manifest concerning this abode, under the crust of this planet.

That specific location has been *hollowed-out* by God, after the conclusion of the Angelic Probationary Period, and prior to the creation of Adam and the beginning of the Mankind Probationary Period. Additionally, that locale has been designed and designated as the *to-be-permanently-confined* residence of the disobedient and rebellious spirit-souls of created creatures. This large hollow is most probably located some distance of depth under the city of modern-day Babylon, which is located within the country of Middle-Eastern Iraq.

This particular upper-level compartment was designed to be as comfortable as God could make an abode of confinement. Moreover, the temporary residents that we shall observe within this locale are only going to be of the disembodied spirit-soul Human Being category. It is not beyond our comprehension to imagine trees, grass, streams of water, and other pleasantries being provided for those who would be spending an extensive amount of time within this locale, until the promised redemption comes to pass.

Understand that God's locale of Heaven was *closed-for-repairs*, ever since Adam's disobedience and his falling prey to the Law of Sin. *(Romans 5:12)* Within all of the

Old Testament accounts, no matter how behaviorally righteous a person might have been, at their departure from the surface of this planet, they were still not allowed to ascend up into the Third Heaven and to be with God. Moreover, that includes the persons of Enoch and Elijah.

Adam's son Abel was possibly the very first spirit-soul Human Being to experience this locale. *(Hebrews 11:4)* Eventually, he would be joined by Noah, Shem, Abraham, Sarah, Isaac, Jacob, Joseph, Moses, Joshua and many others who died in faith not having received the promises. *(Hebrews 11:39)*

The true story that Jesus tells us within the Gospel of Luke finds the beggar Lazarus becoming another resident of *Abraham's Bosom* after his physical death. Though his unpleasant natural life on the surface of planet Earth was ended, Lazarus could still hear, and talk, and feel, and was even comforted, having access to water. *(Luke 16:20-25)* Not so the rich man. His confinement was quite different.

Scriptural study will bear out that the occupants of *Paradise* or *Abraham's Bosom* only had a temporary lease on that locale. Moreover, that lease was due to expire upon the resurrection of Jesus Christ of Nazareth from the dead. The Bible reveals to us that Jesus led captivity captive *(Ephesians 4:8)* when he ascended into heaven. Behaviorally righteous prisoners of Sin from the days of Abel were *Born-Again* within the Citadel of *Hell* and led forth out of that *Nether World* comfort compartment, and into the glories of heaven because of the shed blood of the Lamb of God.

2) Sheol *(in the Hebrew)* . . . Hades *(in the Greek)*:

"And in hell he lift up his eyes, being in torments, and seeth Abraham afar off, and Lazarus in his bosom." *(Luke 16:23)*

The second upper-level compartment within *The Abode of Evil Spirits* or *The Region of the Damned* can also be found within the true story that Jesus is telling to the scribes and the Pharisees, which is recorded within the Gospel of Luke. This compartment within the large location of *The Infernal Regions* is level with, and directly across from, *Paradise* or *Abraham's Bosom*.

This locale is one of four remaining areas, all of which are compartments of suffering and torment, relegated for confinement of rebellious spirit-soul beings categorized as *the damned*. The residents of this locale would also be only spirit-soul Human Beings and not fallen angels or demons.

Even as Lazarus the beggar was carried by the holy angels into *Abraham's Bosom*, *(Luke 16:22)* so also the deceased rich man would be carried by unholy angels into the torment abode of *Hades*.

And even though he is physically dead, and no longer bodily on the surface of planet Earth, within the burning fires of the *Hades* compartment of *Hell* the rich man is still conscious. He can see clearly, and lifting up his eyes he beholds Abraham and Lazarus the beggar standing at a distance. It would appear that sound also carries well even within the citadel of damnation, and without having to yell the rich man can cry out unto Abraham. Capacity to talk, and to hear, and to feel, and to think and reason all seem to be fully functional, even though the rich man is physically dead. *(Luke 16:23-25)* This author is able to deduce that the wicked rich man was not *annihilated* when his life on this Earth was over, but rather went on to suffer the consequences of what obedience to Sin and evil activity produce.

By its very nature fire burns and is quite hot. The rich man testifies that he is **"*tormented in this flame,*"** *(Luke 16:24)* and requests that Abraham send Lazarus with water dripping from his fingers to cool his burning tongue. However, spirit-soul Human Beings that have been disembodied because of physical death do not have the power of flight and are not able to ascend and descend on their own. In fact, any spirit-soul being that finds themselves in a disembodied condition is going to be lacking the privilege of flight. *(Matthew 12:43)* Were that not to be the case the rich man could simply have flown out of the torment compartment of the *Nether World* and over into the comfort compartment of *Abraham's Bosom*. Or better yet, even fly back to the surface of the planet. However, that is not how it seems to work, is it?

Because of the interaction that we can witness going on between the rich man and Abraham and Lazarus, we are able to conclude that this separate compartment of *Hades* would also be an upper-level compartment within the structured levels of damnation. *Abraham's Bosom* and *Hades* seem to be on the same level-plane with one another, having a great-gulf-divide of separation fixed between them. *(Luke 16:26)* Comfort on the one side and fire and torment on the other. Moreover, the residents of both sides seem to be able to observe and hear what is taking place within the opposite locale area.

Contrary to what religious men think and declare, this is the compartment that Jesus of Nazareth was first brought into by unholy angels when he died in my sins and yours, on the cross of Calvary. The rich man had died in his sins, and his residence within this domain was the consequence of that sin. Jesus of Nazareth died in my sins and yours, and his condemnation to this domain was the consequence of what you and I have done. It is both the visual *soundbite* that we have of the prophet Jonah's experience, and the prophetical time declaration of *"three days and three nights"* made by Jesus of Nazareth himself, *(Matthew 12:40)* that gives God the Father the legal basis for redeeming him from the everlasting torment that you and I deserve. Thanks be to the God of all grace!

After his *New-Birth* *(Romans 8:29; Colossians 1:15 & 18; Hebrews 1:5; Revelation 3:14)* Jesus did visit the locale of *Abraham's Bosom* to present himself as the promised redemptive Messiah to all those who had been waiting for him since the days of Abel. But not before being subjected to everything that the torment compartment of *Hades* could throw at him because of my sin and yours.

3) Tartaroo *(in the Greek)* . . . Tartarus *(in the Latin):*

"For if God spared not the angels that sinned, but cast them down to hell, and delivered them into chains of darkness, to be reserved unto judgment:" *(II Peter 2:4)*

"And the angels which kept not their first estate, but left their own habitation, he hath reserved in everlasting chains under darkness unto the judgment of the great day." *(Jude 6)*

Inappropriate sexual activity that crosses over the *species-barrier* is an abomination before a holy God and is strictly forbidden.

In days gone by a holy angel named Lucifer made a very bad decision to rebel against the God of abounding grace—even when given an opportunity to change his mind, remained steadfast in his rebellion. Judgment for his disobedience occurred, and yet he is still at liberty and not bound today in **"everlasting chains under darkness unto the judgment of the great day."** *(Jude 6)*

Also within days gone by, other holy angels generically named **"principalities, powers, the rulers of the darkness of this world, and spiritual wickedness in high places"** *(Ephesians 6:12)* also made very bad decisions to join Lucifer in his bid for power and rebellion against the God of grace. And even when they were given an opportunity to change their minds, they remained steadfast in their disobedience. Judgment for their insistence toward evil occurred and yet they too are not bound today in **"everlasting chains under darkness unto the judgment of the great day."** *(Jude 6)*

However, the above referenced Scriptures reveal to us that there were some **"angels that sinned"**, *(II Peter 2:4)* and that those angels were ultimately cast into this *Tartarus* compartment of *Hell*, and bound up with chains. So, what is it that has occurred that has made such a difference between their consequences?

"That the sons of God saw the daughters of men that they were fair; and they took them wives of all which they chose." (Genesis 6:2)

"There were giants in the earth in those days; and also after that, when the sons of God came in unto the daughters of men, and they bare children to them, the same became mighty men which were of old, men of renown." (Genesis 6:4)

On two separate occasions lord Satan has ordered unholy-fallen-angels that were under his command to come to this earth to openly seduce and cohabitate with willing Human women for the purpose of producing *half-breed* fallen-angelic children carrying unredeemable defiled Human blood. The crux of these actions was to thwart the prophesied Messianic fulfillment of Genesis 3:15. These abominations transpired once before the floodwaters of Noah were upon the face of the Earth, and once again after the worldwide flood of Noah had occurred.

It is this latter abominable sin of forbidden sexual activity between different species of creation (in addition to the original sin of disobedience and steadfast rebellion) that has landed these fallen-angelic ***"sons of God"*** *(Genesis 6:2 & 4; Job 1:6 & 2:1 & 38:7)* into this abode of darkness.

Obviously *foreknowledge* of these activities was in active operation before *The Region of the Damned* was prepared for the Devil and his angels. *(Matthew 25:41)* But the divine quality of *foreknowledge* does not dictate nor determine God's decisions or actions. The character of a loving God ***"beareth all things, believeth all things, hopeth all things, and endureth all things"***, *(I Corinthians 13:7)* and is not lessened even one iota because of what He may see through *foreknowledge* or what He sees or hears in the here-and-now.

Fire is not mentioned as raging within the Scriptural references of this location, but that does not necessarily mean that there is no fire burning there. However, the compartment is shrouded in darkness to be sure. Moreover, the indication is that only these sexually-promiscuous angels are in residence there. No demons of any kind. And no disembodied Human Beings are alluded to in any way.

When the short seven-thousand year Probationary Period for Mankind is concluded *(Romans 9:28)* and the Great White Throne judgment arrives, these inhabitants of this damnation domain will be removed from this locale to receive their final sentence from the Judge, and then be transferred into the giant *Lake of Fire* region that is right across the ***"great gulf"*** that is fixed *(Luke 16:26)* on this same first-floor level of *Hell*.

4) The Bottomless Pit or Abyss:

Before we take a look at the final compartment of the *Lake of Fire*, may we consider this *throat-type*, ***"great gulf,"*** elevator-shaft corridor leading to the lowest of all of the compartments within *The World of Departed Spirits*. This *throat-type* shaft separates the *Sheol/Hades* and the *Paradise/Abraham's Bosom* compartments on the upper-level, and the *Tartaroo/Tartarus* and *Gehenna/Lake of Fire* compartments on the first-floor level. This shaft goes right past them into the basement of *Hell*.

Referred to as being *bottomless* it penetrates deeper into the bowels of the Earth than any of the other compartments. And although we do not know just how deep the depth of the compartment is, it must indeed have a *bottom* somewhere. Otherwise all that is in the compartment would fall out.

"And the fifth angel sounded, and I saw a star fall from heaven unto the earth: and to him was given the key to the bottomless pit.

And he opened the bottomless pit; and there arose a smoke out of the pit, as the smoke of a

great furnace; and the sun and the air were darkened by reason of the smoke of the pit." (Revelation 9:1-2)

"And they had a king over them, which is the angel of the bottomless pit, whose name in the Hebrew tongue is Abaddon, but in the Greek tongue hath his name Apollyon." (Revelation 9:11)

Uniquely described *locust* and *horsemen* demon entities of sorts are the inhabitants of this damnation domain. In a somewhat warlord-like manner, they have a fallen-angelic king that lords over them, whose Hebrew name is Abaddon but he is called Apollyon in the Greek.

Where did these creatures within this abode come from? would be a legitimate question. Are they part of the original constituency of the First Social Order of inhabitants that were the initial creation that was brought forth to populate this planet? Most probably, *yes*. But how did they come to be confined within part of a region that was created by God—but not prepared until the conclusion of the final judgment, concerning the participants of the Angelic Probationary Period? These creatures are certainly not some sort of distorted fallen angelic beings themselves, for they have an unholy higher *Creation Category* angel that rules over them. Their stated purpose is to torment and to slay Human Beings at given points in time. *(Revelation 9:10 & 18-19)*

This particular compartment has a solid gate installed over the *throat-entrance* that prohibits the smoke of the fire and the occupants themselves from escaping. The lock on that gate requires a specific key to unlock and to open it. When that gate opening does occur, smoke from the fire that is within this compartment billows out of the pit and into the atmosphere of this planet. Emerging from the visually protective covering of the smoke, the *demon-locusts* crawl out onto the surface of the planet. *[Please remember that all demonic creatures are disembodied and as such do not have the power of flight. (Matthew 12:43)]* Later on these entities will be followed by the 200,000,000 fire-breathing *demon-horsemen* whose mission is to kill as many Human Beings as they can, under the direction of an additional four other unholy fallen-angels from the Euphrates River. *(Revelation 9:14)*

The exact location of the opening in the Earth's crust that leads directly to the rim of this pit's *throat-entrance* is not mentioned within the Scriptural accounts. But the opening of the locked gate to this compartment and the subsequent escaping of real smoke and demonic creatures from within the pit does occur years before the literal destruction of the city of Babylon. So the two points of either exit or observation concerning this compartment cannot be the same.

At this particular point in time it is unclear where these *demon-locusts* and *demon-horsemen* originally came from and how these very unusual creatures that are indeed demonic, came to be confined within this lowest compartment of *The Region of the Damned*. Abject disobedience concerning their behavior is foundational to be sure, but in what context and capacity is not made clearly known. However, that they are now confined within this abode is a certainty and the hour of their release is drawing nearer with each passing day.

5) Gehenna . . . or The Second Death . . . or The Lake of Fire:

"And the devil that deceived them was cast into the lake of fire and brimstone, where the beast and the false prophet are, and shall be tormented day and night for ever and ever." *(Revelation 20:10)*

The fifth and the final compartment within *The World of Departed Spirits* that was originally **"prepared for the devil and his angels"** is the *Lake of Fire*.

This compartment is the final destination of every non-compliant, rebellious, spirit-soul being from both Probationary Periods. Moreover, any future *is-that-your-final-answer* decisions that may occur, from any free-will moral creatures throughout the universe within the everlasting ahead, will also find their new residence within this *Lake of Fire*.

This is where the buck stops. This is where the fog-horn of finality sounds off on a regular basis as a reminder to all of the inhabitants of this region. There is no appointed *ruler* here. Only a quagmire of seething hatred emanating forth from one resident to another, as wails of pain and hopelessness bounce off of and echo up against the containment parameters, and teeth are heard to be gnashing from behind and within an undulating curtain of fire. The virus of rebellion and self-exaltation is finally being nipped in the bud, with the oozing tip eternally cauterized closed with truth and reality.

This is the last stop. All of the previous visitors to *Abraham's Bosom* have by this time been spiritually *Born-Again* and redeemed from all destruction and condemnation. Jesus himself liberated them and led the majority of them to heaven upon his physical resurrection from the dead. *(Matthew 27:52-53)(Ephesians 4:8)* The compartment of *Paradise* or *Abraham's Bosom* now stands empty and is being absorbed into the whole of the region. *(Isaiah 5:14)*

At the time of the Great White Throne judgment, all of the inhabitants of the *Sheol/Hades* compartment shall be raised up from the dead and become united with their previously occupied physical bodies once again. They shall then stand before Judge Jesus and find themselves part of the damned. *(John 5:22)*

Varying levels of obedience shall equate to varying degrees of reward for the saints of the Most High God. In like manner, varying levels of disobedience shall equate to varying degrees of punishment for adamant rebels. All of the spiritual transgressors that stand before the Judge shall be condemned, and none of them shall be rescued at the last minute and be saved. Subsequently, they will be removed from their locale and reassigned from the spiritual *jail* compartment of *Sheol/Hades* over into the *prison* compartment of the *Lake of Fire* to serve out their eternal sentence.

Upon their being cast into this reservoir of molten torment, their physical bodies shall be burned up and destroyed for the *Second Death* time. *(Revelation 20:14)* The disembodied spirit-soul portion of their being shall then be subjected to indescribable anguish and pain, even as the rich man was experiencing within the true story that Jesus told us. *(Luke 16:23-24)*

For the final one-thousand years of Probational time for Mankind, Satan has been in solitary confinement within the compartment of the *Bottomless Pit*. *(Revelation 20:1-3)* Michael the Archangel bound him with a chain and cast him into this pit to keep him quiet and to arrest the blatant activities of his company *toadies*. With there being no apparent active free-will operating within the kingdom of darkness—when you bind the one that gives the orders, no one else knows what to do. Demons and unholy fallen-angels are being systematically dealt with by the New Creation saints of the Most High God. *(1 Corinthians 6:3)* However, during that process, with no orders being given from the top, there are no orders being received. With no orders being received, there are no foul maneuvers being carried out. There is a genuine suspension of most of the evil activity that is now so blatantly active upon the Earth today.

Upon Satan's release from the *Bottomless Pit* after one-thousand years, that abode becomes the second compartment vacancy within the whole of *The Abode of Darkness*. There are no other spirit beings left contained within the compartment. They were loosed upon the Earth for a specific purpose during the Tribulation Period. Moreover, that purpose now being accomplished, they are in line for eternal sentencing and incarceration within the *Lake of Fire* when the appropriate time comes.

Sexually promiscuous fallen-angels now confined within the compartment of *Tartarus* will also be released at the time of the Great White Throne judgment to receive their final sentencing and incarceration. Upon the decreed utterance and the drop of the gavel, they also will be ushered into the *Lake of Fire* with all of the rest. The *Lake of Fire* compartment within the locale of *Hell* will step-by-step swallow up all of the other compartments as they fulfill their responsibilities until it is singularly one. *(Isaiah 5:14)*

* * *

Consignment to the region of *Hell* has already been pre-determined for the participants of the first rebellion because their time of probation has concluded and general judgment has been rendered, but the creation of free-will Mankind lies directly ahead.

Free-will volition for the finest of all created-creatures to come forth from the hand of God and rebels from a prior uprising continuing to remain free from incarceration and the option of ***"life and death, blessing and cursing"*** *(Deuteronomy 30:19)* being set forth for choice, shall all necessitate the delay of judgmental righteousness incarceration. Free-will decision with eternal consequence of that decision will become manifest with no possibility of objection or complaint.

* * *

The majority of Mankind on the Earth today mocks and ridicules the benevolent Creator of this entire universe. Man stupidly chooses to stumble around scientifically in darkness when God has given intelligent commentary concerning all things. *(II Peter 1:3)* He chooses to grovel in the dirt and behave as if he were an animal concerning the very basics of life. He plugs his ears and shouts as loud as he can in order to drown-out the petitions of love that are being spiritually mailed to him with everything he sees and hears and touches and even more so, what he truly knows deep down within his own heart. *(Romans 1:19)*

Without being able to confirm their own scientific suppositions men launch themselves through the curtain of death with unreasonable expectations that they are going to find peace and tranquility in a make-believe world in which they get to drag all of their garbage with them through the veil. Walking through a white-washed eternity with unrepentant attitudes, mindsets, deceptive beliefs, and ambitions, justified in their positions because of a heart overflowing with abundant oozing carnal *love* for another from within their own *Creation Category*.

But, be extremely careful not to muddy the water of fantasy with Biblical facts. Do not *fall for* the emanations of grace and genuine love in lieu of *scientific evidence*. Remember that there is no good or evil. There is no right or wrong. There is no light or darkness. It is all just one big happy *Circle of Life* where we will all ultimately blend into the stream of eternity as of a glass of water being poured out into the gently flowing river of existence. God in heaven—forgive us.

The Creation of Man

"And the Lord formed man of the dust of the ground, and breathed into his nostrils the breath of life; . . ." (Genesis 2:7a)

The *Basic Creation Element* of *Soil* is the primary ingredient utilized within the formation material that God caressed in the creating of the physical Terrestrial body for a man named Adam, who was the first Human Being that was ever created.

* * *

Special Notation: *Foreknowledge is completely aware of the reality that in just a few thousand years one of the Members of the Godhead is going to put on a physical Terrestrial body that has been prepared for Him,* (Psalms 40:6-10)(Hebrews 10:5) *utilizing the very formation material that originally produced the physical Terrestrial body of the Man named Adam.*

The Second Person of the Godhead will then encapsulate and restrict Himself to all future universal operations, functioning from an upgraded, supernatural, Spiritual model of that same physical Terrestrial body. Consider for just a moment what kind of supernatural ingredients may be originally contained within the Basic Creation Element of Soil at the outset, yea, within all of the original Basic Creation Elements of construction?

THE CREATION OF MAN

* * *

At a predetermined moment in *time*—somewhere within the direction of *the West* *(Genesis 2:8)*—the Holy Spirit of God invisibly gathers together the utterance decrees that have been whispered by the creative Word, in line with, and according to, the desires of the Master Creator, and utilizing the very real substance of faith, glues together the components that make-up a physical Terrestrial body, and manifests a housing which carries the uniqueness of personal Divine design. *(Genesis 1:26a)* This housing is fully *mature* in its developmental status and installed with individual-operational-reproductive-capacity—it is a top-of-the-line model.

Physically manifested *hands, feet,* and *facial* features are installed that mirror the *form* *(Philippians 2:8)* and the *shape* *(John 5:37)* of the Master Creator Himself. And once the unit has been inspected and approved, the Spirit of the Most High God gathers together the summation of the whole of His internal being (lacking of course for the specific non-transferables) and gently exhales into the nostrils of the natural, Express-Image prototype. *(Genesis 2:7a)*

The unit springs into existence-life without any discernible, disruptive, jarring movement. Only upon an abrupt gasping inhale that willingly receives the flowing exhale of the divine, does the creation, and all of the specific functioning components of the prototype unit leap into operation. Custom-designed eyes suddenly flash open and are flooded with the full spectrum of brightness and color. The heart of the unit at the outset is found to be racing, and the respiration operations increased dramatically with the jump-start from a non-existence to the accelerated-pulsating of the granted gifting of *Eternal Life*.

God has literally exhaled every aspect and quality concerning His very own Personage into His MAN without diminishing that Divine Personage even one iota. He has invested Himself to the uttermost. If there were a created creature that could rightfully be called a son of the Almighty God, this would be the one. God's Personage has been replicated in every possible detailed aspect. Only the impossible-impartation of the non-transferables separates the two.

Gently, the functioning Human housing is lifted up and *time*lessly transported into the pristine garden setting that has been lovingly prepared. *(Genesis 2:8b)* Set down upon his feet in an upright manner the newly created **M**anifested **A**nimated **N**eophyte—MAN, aptly named Adam, begins to drink in the beauty and awesomeness of *Life* itself, and slowly begins to take stock of his new surroundings.

He is the delight of Divine desire, and excitement

is high as activities are scheduled for Father and son. Only the qualities of *self-existence* . . . *Omniscience* . . . *Omnipotence* . . . and *Omnipresence* are missing from this one. The Absolute of Light, Life, and Love has peeled off a portion of His very self and by impartation brought forth a carbon-copy, Express Image, of the unduplicatable Divine.

* * *

Special Notation: *What is a spirit?*
Webster's Ninth New Collegiate Dictionary defines "spirit" as . . . 1. *an animating or vital principle held to give life to physical organisms.* 2. *a supernatural being or essence: as* **a)** *cap: Holy Spirit*
b) *Soul* **c)** *an often malevolent being that is bodiless but can become visible; specifically: ghost.*

"God is a Spirit: and they that worship him must worship him in spirit and in truth." *(John 4:24)*

God, who is the only self-existent, omnisciently, omnipotently, and omnipresently operating Spirit being that there is, is the summation of and the totality of all Life within this created universe.

He is the designer and the creator of the entire Realm of the Spirit, and all of the spiritual actions and activities that exist will find their origin within Him.

The Realm of the Spirit is a supernatural realm that functions according to the highest set of creative laws that operate on a standard quantum level.

Additional intelligent, moral, free-willed spirit beings that God has creatively brought forth out of love alone, are the Creation Category #3 – Other Creatures, the Creation Category #2 – Angelic Hosts, and the Creation Category #1 – Mankind, also known of as Human Beings. Of those creations, Mankind carries the supremacy.

* * *

So pleased with His MAN is the Lord, that He anticipatively installs him into an extensively-expansive position of authority which blankets the whole of this universe, excepting only for Himself and His throne. *(I Corinthians 15:27)* However, it is an understood reality that this authority, in its operational manifestation, is progressive because of the necessary requirement of free-will-obedience-substantiation. Should Adam prove to be a good steward over the *little* of the garden, *(Matthew 25:21)* he will then be made to be the steward over the *much* of the planet Earth. Should he become a good steward over the *little* of the planet Earth, he will then be made to be the steward over the *much* of the solar system. Should he become a good steward over the *little* of the solar system, he will then be made to be the steward over the *much* of the Milky Way galaxy. Should he become a good steward over the *little* of the Milky Way galaxy, he will then be made to be the steward over the *much* of the select quadrants of the universe. Should he become a good steward over the *little* of the select quadrants of the universe, he will then be made to be the steward over the *much* of the entire universe. *(Hebrews 2:8)* Moreover, with that clearly established and understood, we shall begin.

* * *

The first stewardship assignment (after his required *orientation* takes place) will be one of maintenance and guardianship. *(Genesis 2:15)* Adam's two-fold task will be to keep the flora and fauna within the garden orderly and trimmed by authoritatively speaking, even as his Father issues His directives forth for all of creation to acknowledge and to adjust to. *(Romans 4:17b)* The garden is specifically there for the benefit and the pleasure of the MAN but during the process of development and growth it needs to be attended to.

Secondarily, the intelligent, free-will, moral constituency of the First Social Order (even though they are all *physically* dead because of floodwaters, and now have become *demons*) are all still here on planet Earth and certain of the fallen angels are hanging around as well. There is no **"veil that we see through darkly"** in place yet *(I Corinthians 13:12)* so those

Creation-Category #2 and #3 creatures are visible to the physical eye, and Adam is to *keep* the garden free from intrusion by outsiders. *(Genesis 2:15b)*

Adam comes short in no area of his being. He has been gifted with a brain for unit-directive-functioning, and a 100% granted capacity usage of it. There are no debilitating effects yet of the Law of Sin to diminish the brain's performance, and so it operates at full throttle.

The totality of the male and female sexual gender accruements that shall be utilized in line with reproductive-permission (and which are innately incorporated within the Master Creator) are transferred in totality and now reside within Adam.

As God is fully a three-dimensional Spirit Being— He has created Adam in a full three-dimensional construct as well. Adam is a living spirit being (with a gifted soul compliment of intellect, emotions, and free-will) living within the likeness-of-God housing that was masterfully put together by the Holy Spirit of grace.

Being that there is no active operation of the Law of Sin working in the Earth at this time, *(Romans 5:12)* Adam is fully able to believe whatever God may say unto him. If it were a requirement, he could walk on the water. If it were a requirement, he could calm a storm. If it were a requirement, he could say to the mountain **"Be thou removed, and be thou cast into the sea;"**

(Mark 11:23) and it should obey him. He is a man of supreme authority without any fear of intimidation or failure, able to speak things *"which be not as though they were."* *(Romans 4:17b)*

* * *

Special Notation: *Day 6 of the whole of the restoration process for planet Earth is the specific day that MAN was originally created . . . it was a Friday, as we note various days in time. The completed-restoration process of the planet Earth now being finished at that particular time . . . Day 7 is designated as a day of rest.* *(Genesis 2:2-3)* God Himself is not fatigued . . . but rather is setting a precedent for both the future prophetical-shadow requirements of law (concerning the Law of Moses) *(Leviticus 16:31)* and the Redemption-Completion-Reality fulfillment of the New Creation. *(Hebrews 4:1)*

* * *

Day 7 begins Adam's *orientation*. Once *orientation* requirements are completed, which included various issued decrees of obedience, then *lab-time* activities can commence. The *Animal* compliment for the Second Social Order is not created and named within a one day's period of *time*. Scripture does not reveal just how long the process took, but rather it simply states that it did indeed take place—it is important to see that the 24-hour *time* notations for activities-accomplished are no longer being made.

The *Tree of Life* is the most uniquely designed, universal product-of-perpetuation within the entire spectrum of all of the created flora and fauna that has ever been brought forth into existence. *(Genesis 2:9b)* Utilizing all three of the divinely-invested *Basic Creation Elements* the Godhead has uploaded into both the leaves of the *Tree* and the fruit that it produces, eternal-sustaining elements of *Life* that have the capacity to counteract a physical-mortality condition and the eternal-death consequence that should come forth because of spiritual deficit.

This *Tree* is originally created, cultivated and fully developed within the foliage compliment of the City New Jerusalem on the planet Heaven. *Foreknowledge* transplants a fully mature candidate of this spectacular example of vegetative life into the Garden of Eden setting, when the garden is first planted by God. Adam is admonished to eat the fruit of this *Tree* before the Law of Sin has an opportunity to ensnare him. *(Genesis 2:16b)* However, he fails to pick-up on this hint and chooses to focus his attention in another direction.

The first scheduled appointment of *lab-time* between Father and son finally arrives. The fatherly love of creation motivates God to express His innermost parental provision and declare, **"It is not good that the man should be alone; I will make him a help**

meet for him. *(Genesis 2:18)* God draws Adam off to a locale within the Garden of Eden and utilizing the *Basic Creation Elements* of the *Water* and the *Soil* begins to create the specifically designed, non-moral, instinctive compliment that is being prepared for the fledgling society that stands on the brink of emergence.

These associate creatures shall ultimately be called *Animals*, and the three-fold purpose that motivates *foreknowledge* in their creation is for companionship, and for burden bearing, and for food and necessary sacrifice, concerning Mankind, when the acidic operation of the Law of Sin spreads like a wildfire across the face of the land.

"And out of the ground the Lord God formed every beast of the field, and every fowl of the air; and brought them unto Adam to see what he would call them: and whatsoever Adam called every living creature, that was the name thereof."
(Genesis 2:19)

One of the first of the *lab-time* activities that occurs between Father and son is the authoritative naming of the animal-compliment that God is creating for this Social Order of Mankind. God creatively designs and then manifests the particular creature of choice, and then His son completes the process by verbally attaching an appropriate name-tag. Specimen after specimen is brought forth and named, but there are ultimately none of them that can be a fitting compliment for the Man named Adam.

"And Adam gave names to all cattle, and to the fowl of the air, and to every beast of the field; but for Adam there was not found a help meet for him." *(Genesis 2:20)*

God has now arrived at a juncture . . .

The planet named Earth has been restored from judgmental necessities to habitational-conformance for the second time.

An unprecedented superior creature of supreme God-class status has been created and installed as the new resident regent of the planet named Earth.

A new associate animal compliment has been created and personally named by the installed resident-regent . . . but something is still lacking.

All-knowingly, God injects the first administration of hypnotic-anesthesia and puts His supreme God-class status prototype into a deep sleep. *(Genesis 2:21a)*

The non-evasive surgical procedure removes a necessary physical *starter unit* that shall be used for the duplication of an already established physical Terrestrial body. *(Genesis 2:21b-22a)*

THE CREATION OF MAN

An invisible doppelganger extraction of unique feminine and dually shared qualities occurs (and a merging of all essential elements takes place resulting in the creation of another MAN) only this one is equipped with breasts and a womb. *(Genesis 2:22b)*

God has now provided a lock for the key to an entire species of potential, universally-authoritative God-class creatures.

When Adam awakens from his slumber he is more than pleasantly surprised. A delighted exclamation of ***"This is now bone of my bones, and flesh of my flesh:"*** *(Genesis 2:23a)* emanates forth from his lips. As he drinks in the uniqueness of the one who is the same as he, and yet so magnificently different, he proclaims ***"she shall be called Woman, because she was taken out of man."*** *(Genesis 2:23b)*

"And they were both naked, the man and his wife, and were not ashamed." *(Genesis 2:25)*

May we please understand at this particular juncture in time that Adam is not ceaselessly, hormonally, salivating at the sight of the Woman. There is no active Sin in operation on this Earth as of yet. There is no manifestation of lust . . . nor of lewdness . . . nor of unclean thoughts . . . nor of the blood-racing hormones of sexual excitement . . . nor of the shame that all demonstrate themselves so clearly in the day and age in which we live where Sin is running amok and the intents of men's hearts is to do evil continually. *(Genesis 6:5)*

The Hope for Man

". . . and let them have dominion over the fish of the sea, and over the fowl of the air, and over the cattle, and over all the earth, and over every creeping thing that creepeth upon the earth." *(Genesis 1:26b)*

Because we are so continually made aware of the failure of Adam and Eve, in their disobedience before God, we give very little thought, if any, to what might have been if they had continued to live within their divine design destiny.

The Garden of Eden was pristine. The grass and the bushes and the trees were all the handiworks of the Master Creator himself. *(Genesis 2:8)* Adam was a brand new **M**anifested **A**nimated **N**eophyte, who was full of spiritual Life. He was unacquainted with the reality of doubt, or of questioning, or of *not* believing. In all probability, God tutored him within his orientation, in speaking forth things that be not, as though they were, *(Romans 4:17)* and believing to receive things that he desired. *(Mark 11:24)*

With this tutorage, Adam's initial attempts at exercising authority were going to be focused upon his ability to keep the grass at an acceptable height and the shrubs and bushes watered and within manicured parameters and the trees vibrant and productive with the flowers and the fruit that they were divinely designed to produce.

When the actual lab-time arrived, God tutored and worked with Adam in a practical, hands-on manner. God led Adam to the water's edge, and spoke forth a divine command to the *Basic Creation Element* of *Water*, and creation of **"every living creature that moveth, which the waters brought forth abundantly, after their kind, and every winged fowl after his kind"** *(Genesis 1:21)* began to come forth as God quietly <u>hastened</u> His **"word to perform it."** *(Jeremiah 1:12)* **"For he spake, and it was done; he commanded, and it stood fast."** *(Psalms 33:9)*

Adam was a quick learner, having 100% brain capacity usage, and in just a short time he was ready to move on to a more advanced lesson.

Back within the meadow portion of the Garden, God directed Adam's attention to the *Basic Creation Element* of *Soil*, **"and God said, Let the earth bring forth the living creature after his kind, cattle, and creeping thing, and beast of the earth after his kind: and it was so."** *(Genesis 1:24)* The <u>hastened</u> word of the Lord responded to the divine command, **"and out of the ground the Lord God formed every beast of the field, and every fowl of the air; and**

brought them unto Adam to see what he would call them: and whatsoever Adam called every living creature, that was the name thereof." *(Genesis 2:19)* ***"For he spake, and it was done; he commanded, and it stood fast."*** *(Psalms 33:9)* ***"And Adam gave names to all cattle, and to the fowl of the air, and to every beast of the field; but to Adam there was not found a help meet for him."*** *(Genesis 2:20)*

Lab-time with the Lord was exhilarating to be sure, and Adam increased his understanding of the power and potential of words backed by faith. He watched intently as God demonstrated the detailed logistics of creation right before his very eyes. The Garden was no longer empty. Beasts of the field were lazily grazing on the meadow. Colorful birds flew from tree to tree, squawking and painting the sky with colorful movement. The waters teemed with fish, and Life was evident everywhere that Adam looked. Conversations between Adam and various creatures within the Garden was interesting, and yet somehow unfulfilling. They were of a different mindset and a different focus. Their affections were not set upon things above. There was nothing of an eternal depth that was able to be exchanged between them, even though the newness of Life swirled everywhere.

Adam loved God, but God was not always there

with him, dwelling within the Garden. Moreover, God's form *(Philippians 2:8)* and God's shape *(John 5:37)* was not even as tangible to him as the animals that were all around him were. Something was missing, and Adam could not quite put his finger on it. He longed for someone who was discernibly more like him, someone who could talk like him and with him as often as he desired, someone who would physically look more like him and with whom he could interact, someone who could think like he thought.

God is a God of Love. And this author believes that one of God's fondest desires is to interact intimately with the finest creation that He has ever made. Foreknowledge is aware of what will ultimately come to pass after the Super-Nova explosion occurrence at the resurrection of Jesus Christ of Nazareth in the millennia ahead. And because Adam is an early prototype, the compassion of the Lord is demonstrated, **"and the Lord God said, It is not good that the man should be alone; I will make him a help meet for him."** *(Genesis 2:18)*

"And the Lord God caused a deep sleep to fall upon Adam, and he slept; and he took one of his ribs, and closed up the flesh instead thereof.

And the rib, which the Lord God had taken from man, made he a woman, and brought her unto the man. *(Genesis 2:21-22)*

And when Adam woke up, the woman was standing there before him in all of her glory. She did not have any spots; her neck was proportional with her body; she did not have a tail swishing behind her, and the smile on her face was enchanting. Her voice was soft and exuded sweetness, and she began to chatter about the freshness of imparted Life that had been recently gifted.

As the days passed, Adam was consumed with finally being able to fellowship with another **M**anifested **A**nimated **N**eophyte—only this one has some complimentary physical differences. At the outset he calls her Woman, testifying to the reality that she really is a MAN, even as he, only she is complimented with a womb, for the purpose of reproducing others of the species.

Adam is enjoying his time with the Woman. He leads her on a guided tour of the Garden and tutors her in the marvels of creation, and the authority and power that God has gifted them both with. The clear admonition that God has given concerning the Tree of the Knowledge of Good and Evil is not first and foremost on Adam's mind, but he casually mentions to the Woman what God had told him. Neither is there a focus on the Tree of Life of which they may freely partake, and by which they would be able to live forever within their Terrestrial physical bodies.

Meanwhile, somewhere along the perimeter of the Garden, Satan finds a weak spot and breaches the hedge-installed boundary. Adam is unaware of the intrusion because of his preoccupation with the Woman; otherwise he would have dealt with him. Satan stealthily works his way further in and encounters the serpent at some point along the way. The serpent knows nothing of spiritual truth and reality because he is a fairly new resident on the scene, among the *beast of the field*. *(Genesis 3:1)* Satan feigns his introduction of who he is and begins to fill the serpent's head with thoughts of exaltation, authoritative position, and promotion to a headship level. The serpent falls prey to the lies and temptation, and an agreement of deception is arrived at between them. Satan confidently retraces his steps and exits the Garden at the same point of original entrance.

The serpent purposes to wander through the Garden and tactfully encounter the twitterpated couple on a regular basis. Casual conversation lays the groundwork for the deception that is planned ahead. At a point in time when he sees Adam and the Woman approaching, he positions himself at a location, within the midst of the Garden, close to the Tree of the Knowledge of Good and Evil. As the lovers draw near . . .

"He said unto the woman, Yea, hath God said,

Ye shall not eat of every tree of the garden?

And the woman said unto the serpent, We may eat of the fruit of the trees of the garden:

But of the fruit of the tree which is in the midst of the garden, God hath said, Ye shall not eat of it, neither shall ye touch it, lest ye die.

And the serpent said unto the woman, Ye shall not surely die:

For God doth know that in the day ye eat thereof, then you eyes shall be opened, and ye shall be as gods, knowing good and evil." (Genesis 3:1-5)

It is at this point that Adam suddenly recognizes that the Woman has uttered ought out of her lips that in incorrect . . . *(Numbers 30:6-8)* but he remains silent. He recognizes that he has dealt frivolously with a very serious issue, but still he remains silent. He has failed to tutor her in depth concerning the preciseness of divine command . . . and compounds that failure by remaining silent.

"And when the woman saw that the tree was good for food, and that it was pleasant to the eyes, and a tree to be desired to make one wise, she took of the fruit thereof, and did eat . . . and gave also unto her husband <u>with her</u> . . . and he did eat." (Genesis 3:6)

No matter what may be preached in modern pulpits today, reality does not change. The woman was deceived, but the man was not deceived. *(I Timothy 2:14)* The woman was in the transgression of disobedience, by the eating of the forbidden fruit. Adam knowingly, willingly, and consciously ate of the fruit without being deceived, and in so doing opened the door for Sin to operate within the world again, and put the actual Law of Sin into the position of lawful ascendency.

Adam consigned himself to spiritual bondage, and the consequence of death, and condemned the entire Human Race that was to emanate forth from him to suffer the same fate, until Jesus Christ of Nazareth would rise from the dead. *(Romans 5:12 & 6:16)*

* * *

Adam and the Woman were originally scheduled to succeed at the Garden of Eden level of the training, concerning obedience and stewardship.

Their promotion would have taken them outside of the Garden and into the chaotic unperfected remainder of the world. The whole of the land was one piece, but conditionally unkempt. The waters were teeming with life, but those creatures within those waters needed to be subdued. Moreover, the fallen moral creation from the previous Social Order, which lived everywhere outside of the Garden of Eden, needed to be handled and controlled, utilizing decreed authority and wisdom.

Adam has already been instructed in the power of words plus faith plus authority. The couple's assignment would be to bring the remainder of this planet named Earth into order and subjection unto the leadership of MAN, thus fulfilling another level of progressive training.

During this process, commanded reproduction would take place *(Genesis 1:28)* and sinless children and grand-children would issue forth and replenish the whole of the planet named Earth with Human Beings and they would be instructed and raised-up in the nurture and admonition of the Lord as the continuing increase occurs.

The solar system to which this planet Earth belongs is not a large one. Successful exercised authority over the Earth would then lead to a graduation and promotion unto the next level of operational stewardship.

Upon the full populous filling of the planet Earth, and the subsequent subjugation thereof, time for colonization would arrive. Moreover, MAN has been made ready to graduate to universal responsibilities. Other stars are approached and other planets explored. Where there is a personal desire, creative vision occurs and the physical realm surrenders to the spiritual authority of the creature that is the *spitting image* of the Creator Himself. Fulfillment of divine heart-desire is occurring regularly.

Had Adam continued in his successful stewardship responsibilities—over expired time—the entire universe that was created by God, would fall under his exercised authority. There were no deadline issues in effect, and God was not at all in a hurry. Effective God and Express-Image Creation would walk hand in hand down the corridor of everlasting, with satisfaction and fulfillment within each heart.

But sadly, that is not what happened . . . is it?

The Deterioration of Man

"But of the tree of the knowledge of good and evil, thou shalt not eat of it: for in the day that thou eatest thereof thou shalt surely die." (Genesis 2:17)

* The Law of Sin did not originate with Adam and Eve, it merely entered back into this world again, by invitation, and revived in its operational activities for a second time. *(Romans 5:12)*

The Law of Sin originally burst forth into existence, and actively manifested onto the scene, when a trusted Holy Angel named Lucifer, *(Ezekiel 28:15)* carrying the anointing of God, *(Ezekiel 28:14)* knowingly, willingly, and consciously acted contrary to, and against, that which he knew to be right and true.

The Law of Sin is the finished product of the vile-ooze of iniquity.

The vile-ooze of iniquity is creatively produced directly from a merging of poisonous *renegade thoughts*, which genesis forth from the soulish portion of the gifted intellect of a moral being, and the equally poisonous *inappropriate personal desires* which emanate forth from the soulish portion of the priceless treasure of free-will. The combining and partaking of these two separate poisons will ultimately prove to be heinously fatal.

The Law of Sin is overwhelmingly compulsive and domineering. *(Romans 7:20)*

The Law of Sin is spiritually corrosive and extremely acidic. *(Romans 6:23a)*

The Law of Sin is unmasked and revealed for what it is by the decreed Law of Moses. *(Romans 7:7)*

The Law of Sin is <u>only</u> able to be effectively dealt with by the precious remission blood of the God/Man Jesus Christ of Nazareth. *(Romans 3:25; Hebrews 9:22 & 10:18)*

Illustratively speaking, the Law of Sin is tantamount to an immense opaque cistern filled with a thick black liquid, which continually drips three varying conditions of the definitive reality of DEATH:

<u>Spiritual Death</u> . . . Which is an invisible universal condition of an entry-level nature. It is that condition of death that originated in this world for a second time with Adam's personal disobedience—and ultimately affected all of Mankind. *(Romans 3:23)* And because of his rebellion, spiritual death has been reproductively passed on down through the ages, to every single Human Being that has ever been born *(Romans 5:12)*, excepting for a man named Jesus Christ of Nazareth. **(Because he did not have a Human father)**

Spiritual Death is odorless, tasteless, and colorless, and it cannot be felt in the natural. It is a fatal, incurable disease for which a loving God has provided an antidote. That antidote is the *New-Birth* of an individual's spirit into an everlasting life condition through the acceptance of the work of the resurrected Jesus Christ of Nazareth.

Physical Death . . . Which is a condition of an abrupt cessation of the physical Terrestrial-bodily functions resulting in non-compliance to the desires or directives of the interior spirit and soul compliment. Physical Death can indeed be felt, and has a bitter after-taste and quite a colorful, but possibly not too pleasant conclusion. It is also a fatal, incurable disease for which a loving God has provided an antidote. That antidote is a physical resurrection and a transitioning into, of an upgraded model of a brand new spiritual-body *if* there is a co-operative, simultaneous working with the spiritual *New-Birth* of the individual unto everlasting life.

Eternal Spiritual Death . . . Which is a condition that is very consequencelly-visible (an advanced-level condition of death) that ultimately becomes the final resting place of tormented spiritual Human Beings. It is an eternal, fatal, locked-down, heinous, incurable disease for which no antidote has been made available nor even exists. Continual abject resistance to pleas of love and offers of redemption have sealed the vile final result of unending fiery torment of wailing and gnashing of teeth within a caldron of continual horror. Each particular Human moral creature has been allowed to go where they have purposely chosen to go, even if they are extremely disappointed when they finally get there. They definitely will not like it, but they did regretfully, knowingly, consciously, and willingly choose it. *

The physical *Remission Blood* of Jesus Christ of Nazareth disintegrates all spiritual, personal sin upon contact, working with the activation of the miraculous *New-Birth* process which occurs by faith. The full storage build-up of Sin's personal-vile-sludge inventory from the time of one's physical birth and entry into this world is completely eradicated, and there is nothing of a destructive nature that remains attached to one's personage. *(II Corinthians 5:17-18)*

With the entrance of the Law of Sin, for a second time, into the active operations of the planet Earth, the magnificent newly-created race of Human Beings begins a downward spiral into the bottomless pit of evil and degeneration. Sin is extremely adhesive and becomes attached to all thoughts, words, and deeds that are allowed to detour from the path of holiness and righteousness. The devastating influence of Sin's power begins as a trickle, and in within a relatively short period of *time* turns into a torrent of darkness. *(Genesis 6:5)*

THE DETERIORATION OF MAN

* * *

Adam has been fully instructed verbally by God, during his *orientation* process and has now become accountable for his actions. *(Genesis 2:17)*

Adam has successfully passed his first *lab-time* activity of the naming of the *Animal compliment* to this current Second Social Order here on planet Earth. *(Genesis 2:20)*

Adam has also successfully executed (to the best of his ability) his instructions to keep the Garden of Eden neat and trimmed and free from any outside invasion or intrusion by unholy-fallen angels or demons. *(Genesis 2:15)* He has had no direct contact or confrontation with any of them.

Adam has recovered from his invisible, surgical, maneuver and summarily received his gifted helpmeet-companion-compliment that he calls Woman. *(Genesis 2:21-23)*

Adam is delighted with his new helpmeet, and they unashamedly enjoy the blessings of the manicured garden setting that they find themselves living in. *(Genesis 2:25)*

Adam was fully instructed by God—because he legally belonged to God—and God carried the responsibility of tutorage.

The woman was created for (and now legally belongs to) Adam. *(I Corinthians 11:9)* Therefore, Adam carries the responsibility of tutorage. In this particular responsibility—Adam fails.

Adam is unaware of Satan's successful entrance into the Garden of Eden, and his seduction of the most subtle of all of the beasts of the field that have only recently been created. *(Genesis 3:1)*

The Word of God is directly assaulted as the subtle-serpent poses a question within a conversation that ensues between he and the Woman—and her response within that conversation—is to her, unknowingly inappropriate. *(Genesis 3:2-3)*

The subtle-serpent has succeeded in baiting-the-trap. He has seduced the Woman into an ***"ought out of her lips"*** declaration. *(Numbers 30:6)*

Adam is not unknowledgeable of the truth and is aware that her statement is in error, but he says nothing. *(Numbers 30:7)* He has failed in his tutorage responsibilities, and he now knows it—but he remains silent.

The subtle-serpent presses the issue and directly lies to the couple. *(Genesis 3:5)*

Focus upon the natural is emphasized, temptation is applied, and uncorrected errant thought coupled with inaccurate word, was followed by inappropriate deed. The Woman was deceived and took of the fruit and did eat. She transgressed against the established ordinance of God. *(1 Timothy 2:14)*

For whatever reason that may be preached in today's world, Adam followed suit. The Woman extended the fruit in hand, and even though he knew better, Adam received and partook of it. He was not deceived. *(I Timothy 2:14)*

The Deed Is Now Done! Sin Has Been <u>Invited</u> Back Into This World!

Spiritual eyes are now open (the shame and guilt that Sin begets arrests the attention of Adam and the Woman) and they attempt to cloak the reproductive portions of their physical Terrestrial bodies as if to protect future generations from the error that they have just committed. *(Genesis 3:7)*

The Genesis accounts will continue to demonstrate a departure from holiness and righteousness, and a further exploration into the dark regions of rebellion.

* * *

An invisible membrane begins to descend and settle upon the planet Earth. (I Corinthians 13:12) The viable Realm of the Spirit and the Realm of the Natural will now suffer a temporary visible/invisible separation because of this membrane, until the "Sin Problem" can be definitively dealt with by God, and the prophesied Millennial Reign of Christ begins.

***

Adam is no longer actively **Eternal** within his personage. He has transitioned into the State of **Mortal** because of Sin and the Death conditions that Sin automatically exudes begin to take hold.

Adam is no longer three-dimensional within his construct. He has now experienced the entry-level ***Spiritual Death*** condition and has become two-dimensional in his activities, operations, and mindset. He has lost a primary dimension portion of his being due to ***Spiritual Death***.

Adam's 100% brain capacity usage will now begin to diminish steadily because of the effects of Sin. Moreover, with every successive generation that comes forth that percentage of usage will be reduced.

Adam's physical Terrestrial body now has a *time-allotment* allocation that is attached to it because of Sin, and physical deterioration will steadily take place up until the time of cessation of bodily response.

* Because of Sin, the activity of sleeping will now become a requirement for muscle rejuvenation and regular physical-battery-recharging.

The action of sleep will move an individual from the condition of being viably conscious and mentally alert, into a condition of being dreamily unconscious.

An individual can exercise sustainable mental *control* while in the viable state of consciousness and mental alertness. However, an individual is unable to exercise sustainable mental *control* while in the dreamily unconscious/sleep condition.

Within Humanity, for many people, a dream is a very, very real occurrence; and yet at the same time, it is not. There is not a lot of intelligent information concerning the *dream-world* for people to learn from. Fantasy fulfillment, supernatural abilities realized, victorious confrontations, as well as fearful anxiety, dashing of hopes, and situations of terror, are experienced. A proposed definition of a dream emanating forth from the *dream-world* would be:

A product from the activity of the Human mind, in an unconscious state, manifesting data input from the five physical senses; without the assurance of whether it will be good or bad. It is the end product of what you are not aware of, that you are unconsciously focusing upon.

Thus, the Realm of the Spirit can interface with the Realm of the Natural utilizing the activity of unconscious/sleep. *

* * *

Adam is now indiscriminately subject to continual temptation being whispered into his thought life, and interwoven into his word utterance, and compulsively applied to his action fulfillment, from the invisible Realm of the Spirit and the unholy, rebellious creatures that currently inhabit that Realm.

Adam is now a spiritual captive within the Realm of the Natural. And with each passing day he is further compelled to become more and more *familiar* with the Natural Realm. Physical sight and physical sound, along with smell, taste, and touch become more and more persuasive and convincing as concerning all of the issues of physical life. Physical life's various activities and the day to day issues of fulfillment thereof repetitively rise up and attempt to overwhelm the actual truth and the genuine spiritual reality that exists.

Adam and Eve are invited to depart from the Garden of Eden in a protective move to shield the Tree of Life from usage fulfillment. Somewhere outside of the garden they begin the fulfillment of the mandate to *replenish the earth (Genesis 1:28)* and their sons of Cain and Abel are born unto them.

The years steadily tick on by, and on a certain given year, when the time of required sacrifice unto God arrives, the elder of the sons, Cain, decidedly leans to his own understanding and chooses to sidestep clearly given instructions, and then attempts to do things his own way. The bringing unto God of sacrificial products that come from a cursed ground . . .

in order to atone for that very same curse . . . is decreed not acceptable, and even though he is admonished to correct his error, his response is one of persistent disobedience that ultimately leads to murder. *(Genesis 4:3-8)* The Covenant-Legalities-Instruction from God that resulted in the life-giving *Shedding-of-Blood Issue,* that was begun within the Garden of Eden setting, *(Genesis 3:21)* is fulfilled by obedient Abel but challenged by a disobedient Cain, and ultimately results in Abel's death.

Sin increases its foothold upon the earth and subsequent to the rebellion of Cain and the death of Abel; a curious spiritual reality emerges. Adam begets a son **in his likeness, and after his image**—just the opposite of what God originally decreed. *(Genesis 1:26 & 5:3)* Because of the effects of the Law of Sin, no longer is the interior portion of an individual, that which is the most important, but rather now it is the outer visible, physical man that demands the primary attention. The era of the *Beautiful People* begins.

Many other sons and daughters are born unto Adam and Eve after their departure from the Garden of Eden. *(Genesis 5:4)* The fact that we are not Scripturally informed of them right away, but rather are become privy to the focused incident of Cain's rebellion, does not change the reality of it.

Cain separates himself from the Lord and his

parents and marries one of his sisters, or a niece, and they began their family. *(Genesis 4:16)*

Cain and potentially other brothers working with him build a city and name that city after Cain's firstborn son. *(Genesis 4:17)* *(The idea of one man building an entire city by himself, or of an entire city being built just for the immediate family of one man, does not even make any sense.)*

Subsequent to the rebellion of Cain and the death of Able, sin dramatically increases its foothold upon the earth. Men and women actively reproduce, and the development of the Human Race increases exponentially.

At a given point in time, Satan deduces that he is going to need to do something drastic to thwart the declaration that God had made concerning a Redeemer for Mankind. *(Genesis 3:15)*

Satan commands certain subservient fallen-angels, which look like men in their appearance, to leave their angelic habitation, and abandon their first estate, and come to dwell on the planet Earth. *(Jude 6)*

Their marching orders are to approach, seduce and wed Human women, for the purpose of developing an entire constituency of unredeemable, half-fallen-Angelic and half-Human Being children. *(Genesis 6:2)* Presentation of themselves as being gods and the promise of making any Human women who would be willing to cooperate with them a goddess becomes very tempting.

Since there are no female angels in existence, there is no x-y chromosome issue in operation. All of the children that shall be born of these Human women will most certainly be male. They shall be supernatural in their prowess *(II Peter 2:11)* and be able to defeat all natural Human males in any combat issue that may arise. Because they are half-Human, they carry all of the authority that God has given unto Mankind. *(Genesis 1:28; Psalms 8:4-8; Hebrews 2:8)*

This is a really good plan from *Hell's* point of view, and before too much time goes by we should be able to build quite an army of blood-line defiled Human Beings, that shall become servants of Satan forevermore. No Redeemer for Mankind will be able to come forth because of unredeemable blood-defilement. The Human Race will become an authoritative Superior set of creatures, with which we shall be able to control the universe.

Violation of sexually crossing-over of species-barrier lines brings arrest and incarceration of these transgressing angels. *(II Peter 2:4)* Their influence, and the influence of their children, only adds to the growing wickedness that is swallowing up Mankind through the proliferation of Sin. Because the blood-defilement has become so pronounced, God must intervene to preserve the Human Race.

Warnings concerning a worldwide flood are given,

(Genesis 6:5-8) and a man who is still **"perfect in his generations"** *(Genesis 6:9)*, by being undefiled in his bloodline, is called upon to build an ark to the saving of his household.

Through a man named Noah, and his three sons, God successfully preserves the precious creature that was His finest project ever.

* * *

Although during the days of God's building of the Nation of Israel, the **"and also after that"** *(Genesis 6:4) was put into effect by Satan to attempt a second thrust in prohibiting the Messiah for that nation to come forth. The results of that effort started with the giants in the "Promised Land" even unto after the David and Goliath conflict. Today, there are not any of the products of that fallen-angelic reproduction left on the Earth.*

Fallen Man's Condition Today

"For God so loved the world, that he gave his only begotten Son, that whosoever believeth in him should not perish, but have everlasting life." (John 3:16)

At the outset of this chapter may we understand that approximately two-thousand years ago, God intervened into the affairs of Man, and provided an opportunity for any Human Being that would desire to escape destruction, to be ultimately preserved unto eternal Life forevermore. A two-thousand-year window of escape, within a seven-thousand year total Probationary Period, has been made available for **whosoever** dwelleth upon the Earth.

A commission of mandate has been issued by the Redeemer of Mankind himself to make sure that the entire world is made aware of this gracious provision. *(Mark 16:15-18)*

World-wide cultural upbringing conditions, combined with promotion of profusely false *religion*, and a general refusal by most of those who are redeemed, to carry out this mandate, has resulted in a massive amount of rejection of the truth and increased development of fantasy belief, which will ultimately result in incalculable destruction and devastation of precious Human souls that God Himself desires that none should perish. *(II Peter 3:9)*

That being said, what is the current Human condition on this planet and what does the Holy Scripture reveal lies just ahead?

* * *

The *in particular* nuances of that which is generally the same on a global scale, concerning the activities of Sin, both seen and unseen, this author may not be totally aware of. However, sinful Human Beings are still going to think, talk, and act like sinful Human Beings. So there is really nothing new under the sun, even as King Solomon said so many years ago. *(Ecclesiastes 1:9)*

Moreover, within the United States of America, the Western culture's icon of prominence, the workings of observable Sin can be clearly discerned.

Within the unseen (and thought to be undetectable realm) jealousy still rages and produces violence, hatred, animosity, and inappropriate activities of all kinds. The Scripture itself reveals just some of the workings of Sin.

"The works of the flesh are manifest, which are these, adultery, *which is inappropriate sexual activity by a married person, with someone outside of their marriage* covenant, **fornication,** *which is inappropriate sexual activity by individuals outside of any marriage covenant,* **uncleanness,** *which is whatsoever is opposite of purity, including sodomy, homosexuality, lesbianism, beastiality, and all other forms of inappropriate sexual perversion,* **lasciviousness,** *which is the promoting of, or partaking of, that which tends to produce lewd emotions, and anything that tends to foster lust, inappropriate sex, or sin,*

Idolatry, *which includes image worship and anything on which affections are passionately set,* **witchcraft,** *which is sorcery and the practice of dealing with evil spirits, including magical incantations and the casting of spells and charms upon someone by means of drugs and potions of various kinds,* **hatred,** *which is bitter disdane, abhorrence, malice, and ill-will against anyone,* **variance,** *which is dissensions, discord, quarreling, debating, and disrupting,* **emulations,** *which are jealousies and striving to excel at the expense of another, including uncurbed rivalry in the areas of religion, business, society, and other fields of endeavor,* **wrath,** *which is turbulent passions, domestic and civil turmoils, rage, and determined and lasting anger,* **strife,** *which is disputations, janglings, and contentions about words, or contesting for superiority or advantage, including strenuous endeavor to equal or pay back in like, the wrongs done unto you,* **seditions,** *which is popular disorder in stirring up strife in religion, government, home, or any other place,* **heresies,** *which simply refers to a doctrinal view or belief at odds with the recognized and accepted tenents of* *a system, church, or party,*

Envyings, *which is pain, ill-will, and jealousy at the good fortune or blessing of another,* **murders,** *which is to premeditatively kill a person or to spoil or mar the happiness of another,* **drunkenness,** *which is a life style of living intoxicated, participation in drinking bouts, and, in truth, being a slave to drink,* **reveling,** *which is lascivious and boisterous feastings and carousing, with obscene music, and other sinful activities,* **and such like. Of the which I tell you before,** *even* **as I have also told you in time past, that they which** *involve themselves and* **do such things** *as these,* **shall not inherit the Kingdom of God."**
(Galatians 5:19-21 — Enhanced)

The very obvious and small cadre of commonly known activities that the majority of the people believe are sinful . . . are smoking, drinking, drug addiction, inappropriate sexual activity, and notorious, riotous living in general. These offenses are not simply relegated to the pagan heathens but include some *saved* individuals as well, who continue to remain carnally minded and regularly yield to the lust of the flesh.

The truly, honest, purpose behind smoking tobacco is to publically *fit-in* and to *impress* other persons. There are no actual positive or beneficial results coming forth from the habit of smoking of tobacco in any form, and the subsequent polluting of the body that most certainly takes place. However, addiction will occur, and the compulsion to satisfy that addiction and lust will override any feeble attempts to quit. Within the days in which we live there are programs that have been developed which have proven successful. But usually the desire to continue to Sin rather than make every effort to cease proves to be the case. Social acceptance of smoking is certainly a precursor to alcohol consumption, drug, and revelry activities designed by the abode of *Hell* itself to debilitate a Human Being and bring them further and further into the bondage of Sin. Tobacco addiction is the *entry-level "Venus fly-trap"* as far as being the unsuspected and unrecognized target from an unseen realm of darkness.

The truly, honest, purpose behind the drinking of alcoholic mixtures of any kind is to numb and slow the functions of the normally conscious mind and the physical senses of the body. The proposed idea that it tastes so good, and that that particular quality gives it its validity is ludicrous. The normal *self-defense* mechanisms installed within the Human Being by God are adversely affected and rendered substandard in their performance. Societal acceptance of alcoholic consumption is an additional precursor to drug and revelry activities, again designed by *Hell* to debilitate and weaken a Human Being and bring them even further into the bondage of Sin. Alcoholic addiction is an unsuspected and unrecognized focused target from an unseen realm. Hopefully, *(from the drunken participants point of view)* in certain circumstances, consumption of alcohol may lead to lustful, uninhibited, liberated, improper, sexual behavior. Oh Boy!

The truly, honest, purpose behind all revelry *(which is lascivious and boisterous feastings and carousing, with obscene music, and additional sinful activities)* is to numb and slow the functions of the normally conscious mind and the physical bodily senses. Again, normal *self-defense* mechanisms installed within the Human Being for a valid reason are adversely affected and rendered substandard in their performance. Social acceptance is the primary focus, and substance addiction is an unsuspected and unrecognized target from the unseen realm of the spirit's point of view. These activities are designed by the workings of *Hell* to debilitate and subdue a Human Being and bring them further and further into the darkness and bondage of Sin. Hopefully, *(from the dumbed-down participants point of view)* in given circumstances, consumption of alcohol, smoking of various substances, and obscene music may lead to desired uninhabited, lustful liberation and improper, sexual behavior. Wow!

The truly, honest, purpose behind illegal drug substance-abuse is to dull and suspend the functions of the normally conscious mind and the physical senses to experience a *buzz* or a *high*. Normally operating *self-*

defense mechanisms purposely installed within the Human Being are adversely affected and rendered substandard and ineffectual in their performance. Social acceptance is now a primary focus of the storm troopers of *Hell* and substance addiction is still the purposed target from the Unseen Realm of the Spirit. Spiritually dull and physically debilitated individuals, whether saved or unsaved, consume alcohol, smoke various substances, contort to loud or obscene music and are actively seeking to become involved in lustful, uninhibited, liberated, improper, sexual behavior. Let's smoke . . . let's get drunk . . . let's do drugs . . . and let's have lots of sex! Yahoo! Let's see how low to an animal level we can go. Sounds just like the cities of Sodom and Gomorrah does it not?

What can be done? Yea, what should be done?

The **only** viable hope that Mankind now has, is found within The Personage of Christ, which is our next study.

"But when the fulness of the time was come, God sent forth his Son, made of a woman, made under the law,

To redeem them that were under the law, that we might receive the adoption of sons." *(Galatians 4:4)*

From the time of Adam and Eve, Mankind was

totally estranged from God because of Sin. At a given point in time, God entered into a legal contract with an idolatrous, pagan, heathen man. God then built an entire people for Himself using that one man. God additionally promised to save the peoples that He had built from the ravages of Sin. God kept His promise to His people and sent a Member of the Godhead to become a Man—that Man was named Jesus of Nazareth, and he was the actual **Christ** or the anointed of God. The **Christ** took it upon himself to pay an incalculable debt that he himself did not owe and now, the only hope that any member of Mankind has is to accept the payment that was made on his behalf by that man. The Man Jesus said,

"I am the way, the truth, and the life: no man cometh unto the Father, but by me." (John 14:6)

Additionally, the Man Jesus said,

"For God so loved the world, that he gave his only begotten Son, that whosoever believeth in him should not perish, but have everlasting life." (John 3:16)

For any Human Being, who surrenders to the petitioning of a loving God, a glorious everlasting future awaits them.

A determined effort should be made to discover everything the Word of God declares concerning who you now are *In Christ*. A purposed *pressing-in* to learn these truths and then a work-plan to put them into practice should occur. Victory and spiritual success will not just happen automatically. God has done His part, and now we need to do ours.

Refusal to accept that which is priceless and yet free, from an extended hand of love, ultimately consigns that Human Being to the consequence of Sin and all of its repercussions.

Choose wisely! Accept that which **Christ** has done. Maranatha!

Meet the Author

By-The-Book Ministries, Inc. began in 2001 as a teaching outreach. Rob E. Daley has been gifted by God to be able to explain biblical truths in an easy to understand manner.

Many have been blessed by his teaching style.

Rob was saved and filled with the Holy Spirit in 1978 and has been instructed by the greatest teacher of all—the Spirit of Truth Himself. Rob is an ordained minister with the Assemblies of God International Fellowship and has pastored in various churches over the past 34 years.

It is the desire of this ministry to see the body of Christ solidly taught, and grow up into the things of the Lord. Rob is available for seminars, retreats, conventions, etc.

Rob can be reached at:

thedaleys@bythebookministries.org

http://robdaleyauthor.com

www.ingramcontent.com/pod-product-compliance
Lightning Source LLC
Chambersburg PA
CBHW032149040426
42449CB00005B/456